CATS FROM AWAY

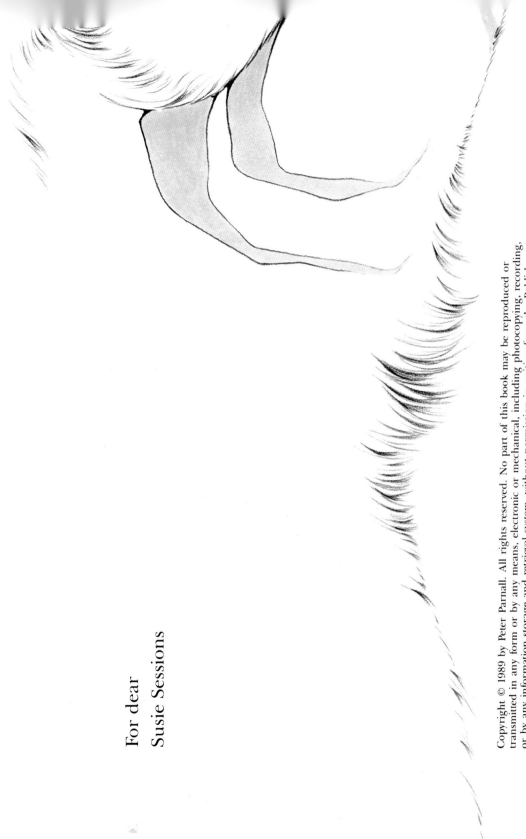

For dear
Susie Sessions

Macmillan Publishing Company, 866 Third Avenue, New York, NY 10022. Collier Macmillan Canada, Inc.
First Edition   Printed in Singapore
The text of this book is set in 14 point Baskerville. The illustrations are rendered in pencil and watercolor.
10   9   8   7   6   5   4   3   2   1

Library of Congress Cataloging-in-Publication Data
Parnall, Peter. Cats from away/by Peter Parnall. – 1st ed.   p.   cm. Summary: Describes the unique characteristics of nine cats who have come to a Maine barn "from somewhere else." ISBN 0-02-770150-6
1. Cats—Juvenile literature. [1. Cats.] I. Title. SF445.7.P37   1989   636.8—dc19   88-30532   CIP   AC

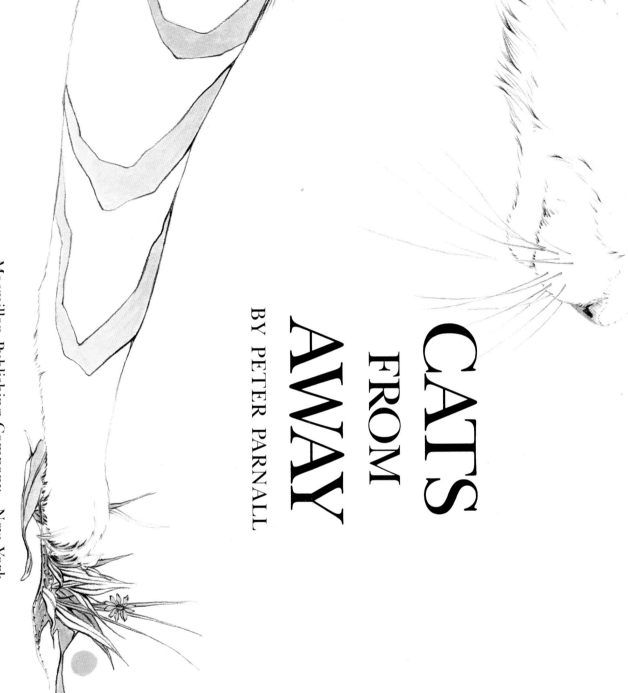

CATS
FROM
AWAY

BY PETER PARNALL

Macmillan Publishing Company   New York
Collier Macmillan Publishers   London

A few cats were born here, but most were brought here or wandered in from somewhere else. From unknown places. From Away. Some were abandoned by thoughtless souls who couldn't be bothered to care or feed. They were dropped off at the end of the lane in hopes that *we* would care and accept them into our small farm's world. Everyone knows that barns have cats. Barns *need* cats. Some barns have too many cats—ours does. Some cats are smart, some are dumb. Some are mean, some are kind, some are quiet, many are loud. Very few are merely *there*. They always make sure that we are aware that they are there. They talk when they are hungry, stomp stiff-legged through barns when they don't get their way, and sometimes find a new, hidden entry to the storage shed, where they carefully slice up garbage bags, spreading the remains of last week's lobster bake evenly over the floor. Artistically, of course. This book is about some of those cats.

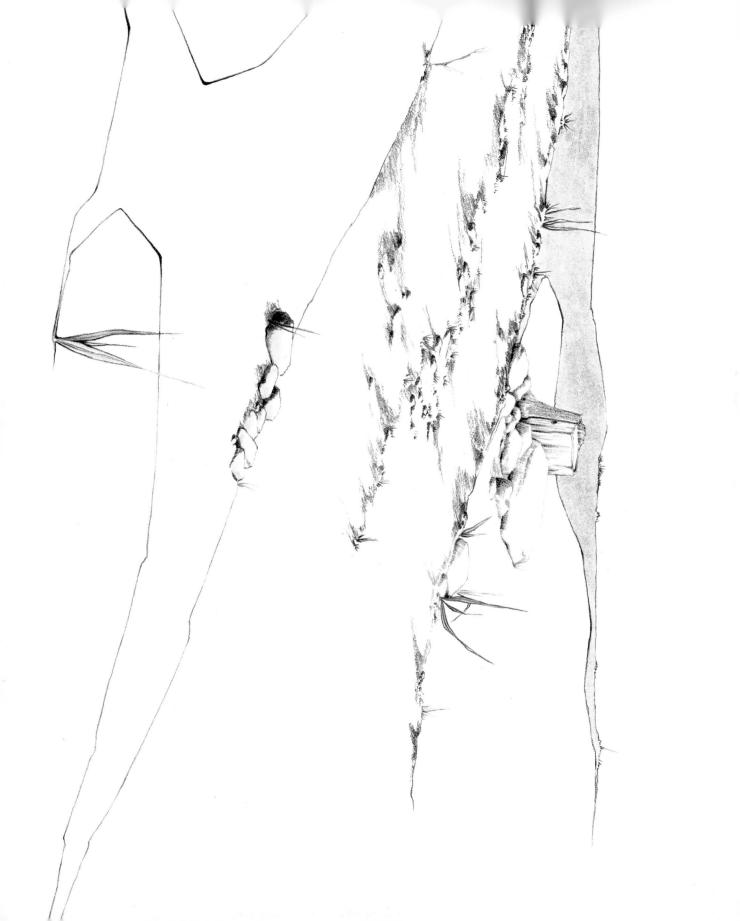

BURL

Burl was born a wild city cat. He hunted alleys by night and subways by day, making a bare living off rats, mice, and garbage-can fare. Far beneath the more pleasant levels of city life he lived, hunted, and fought the years away till the day I found him, a living skeleton heaped behind a refuse can. As my fingertips touched the scarred old head, his engine turned on with a great rumbling *purr*. I wondered if those bones could be a cat again. In a discarded shopping bag I took a discarded cat home. Home to the country.

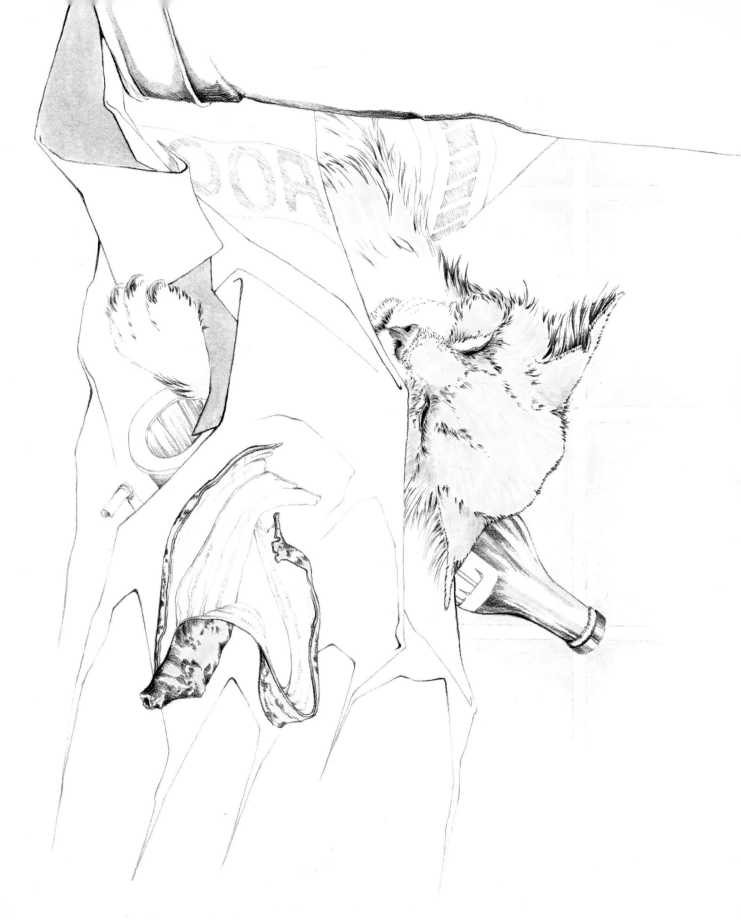

Burl ate and hunted, hunted and ate, gained weight, and ruled the roost...and the barn...and the house...and the hill. At eighteen pounds there were none who challenged his claim to the territory. Sun, fields, woodlands, and a constant urge to explore restored Burl to the best of health. He had many children before passing on, and the last of these was one called Ives.

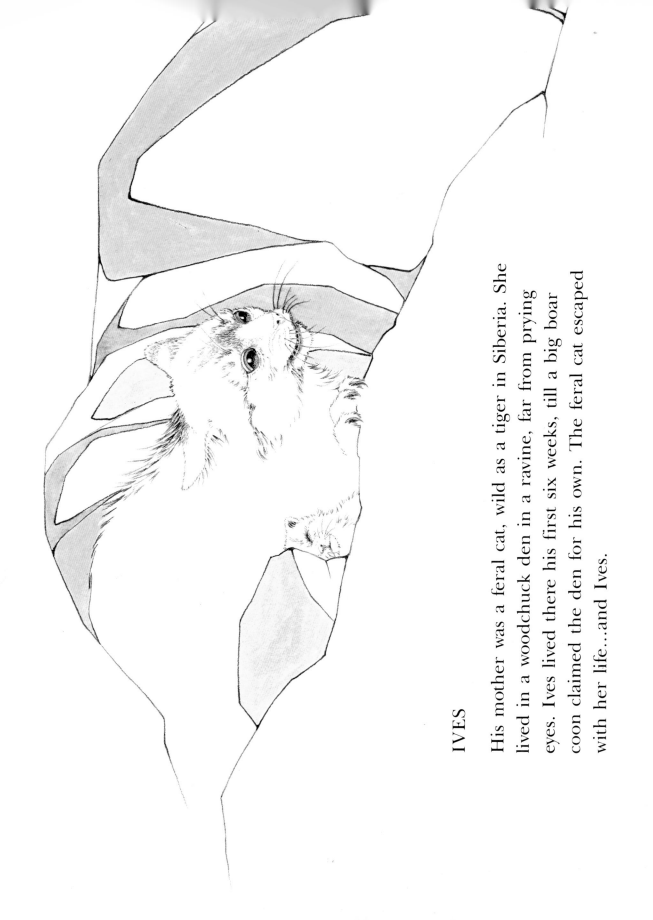

IVES

His mother was a feral cat, wild as a tiger in Siberia. She lived in a woodchuck den in a ravine, far from prying eyes. Ives lived there his first six weeks, till a big boar coon claimed the den for his own. The feral cat escaped with her life…and Ives.

We saw her trot across the drive one night, Ives held loosely in her jaws. Burl's kitten! We called out. Terrified, she dropped her load and flew frantically back to the safety of the ravine. Burl's kitten! A treasure for us. The feral cat was a shadow there...there beyond the barn. Or there...behind the springhouse. A movement, no more. For months we saw only movements and shadows as she watched us raise her kitten. Once she came near enough to steal some food from the barn cats' dish. She never asked Ives to come back to the ravine. He lived with us for sixteen years.

SPITZU

A noisy, Siamese, parrot-loving cat rescued from a shelter and a gruesome end by a two-dollar bill and a sheepish grin. "Of course we all need an extra cat!"

Especially one whose eyes shout from dark corners of a smelly cage: "Help me, please."

Every morning she perched on a kitchen chair, stretched and purred a parrot song as Beckett the bird preened her clean. As clean as a cat could ever be.

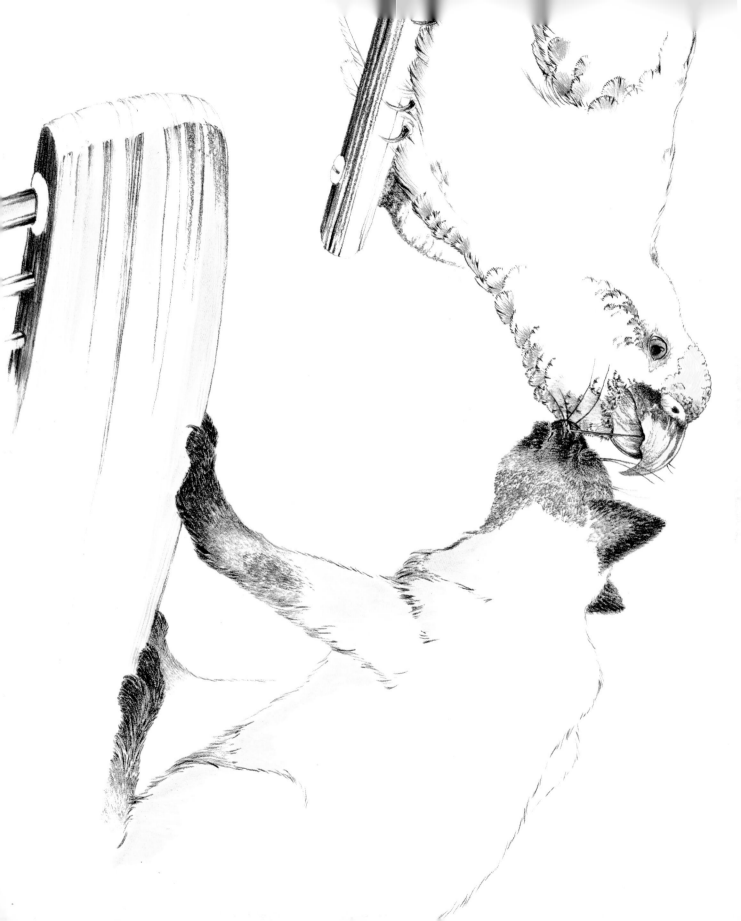

TIGGER

Tigger was a tiger tom who found a fire on a cold January night. He carefully picked his way over thinly crusted snow and sat just outside the ring of light, watching us warm our skates and cook marshmallows on long willow sticks. He was a timid soul, but hunger pulled him toward an outstretched hand that offered food and warmth on that blue, brittle night. We brought him home to our warm, dry barn, and for his remaining years he carefully stayed out of Winter's way. He would have liked Florida.

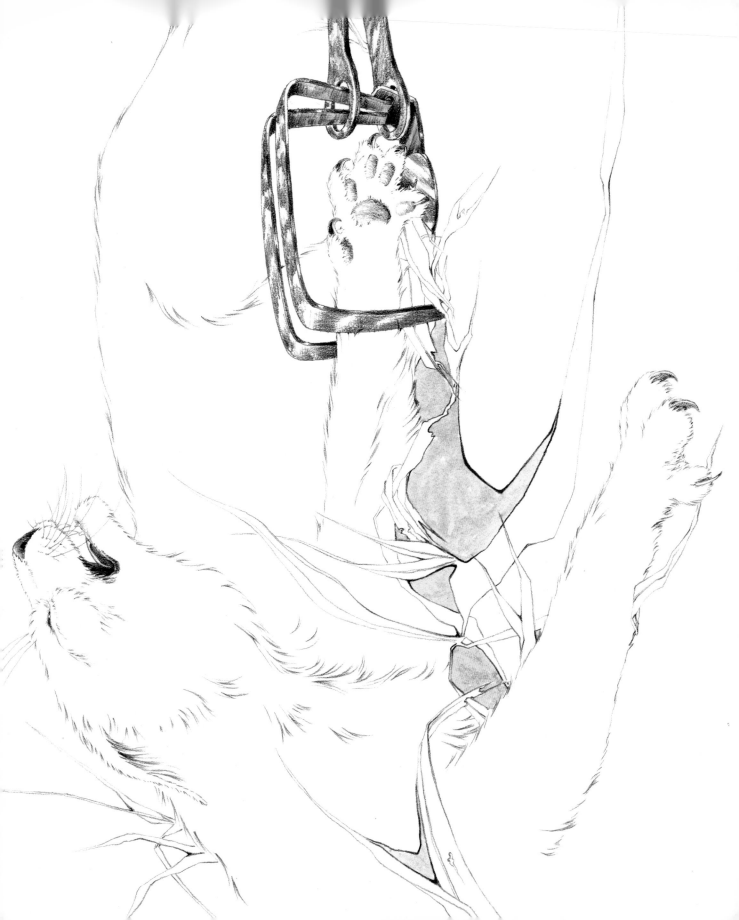

CUD

On a hunting trip in the dark spruce wood he lost his leg in a hunter's trap when he was just a lad of three. Once recovered, he was still the best hunter on the farm, and gave lessons each day to half-grown cats and to kittens, too…generations and generations of kittens.

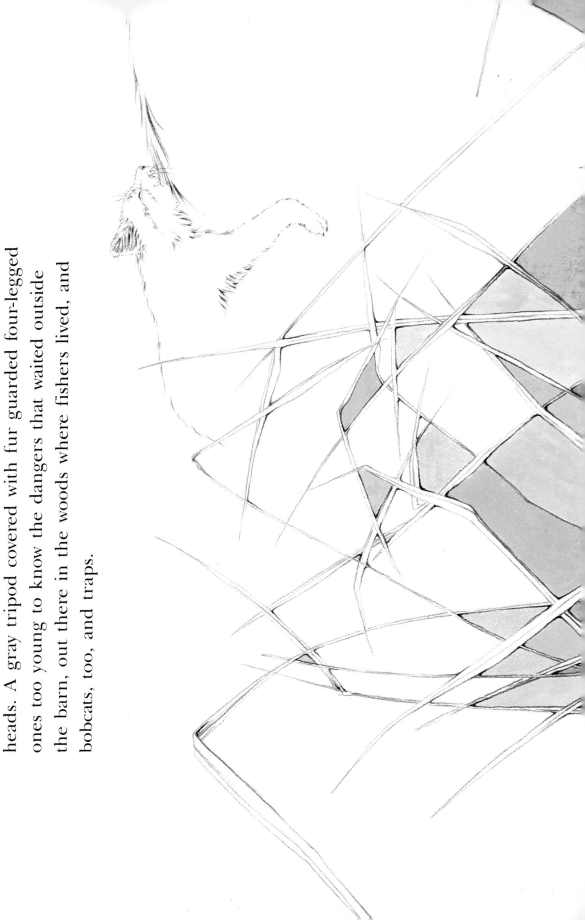

Uncle Cud, big gray Cud, cared for all who needed a bath, who needed a romp, or a soft pillow to warm their heads. A gray tripod covered with fur guarded four-legged ones too young to know the dangers that waited outside the barn, out there in the woods where fishers lived, and bobcats, too, and traps.

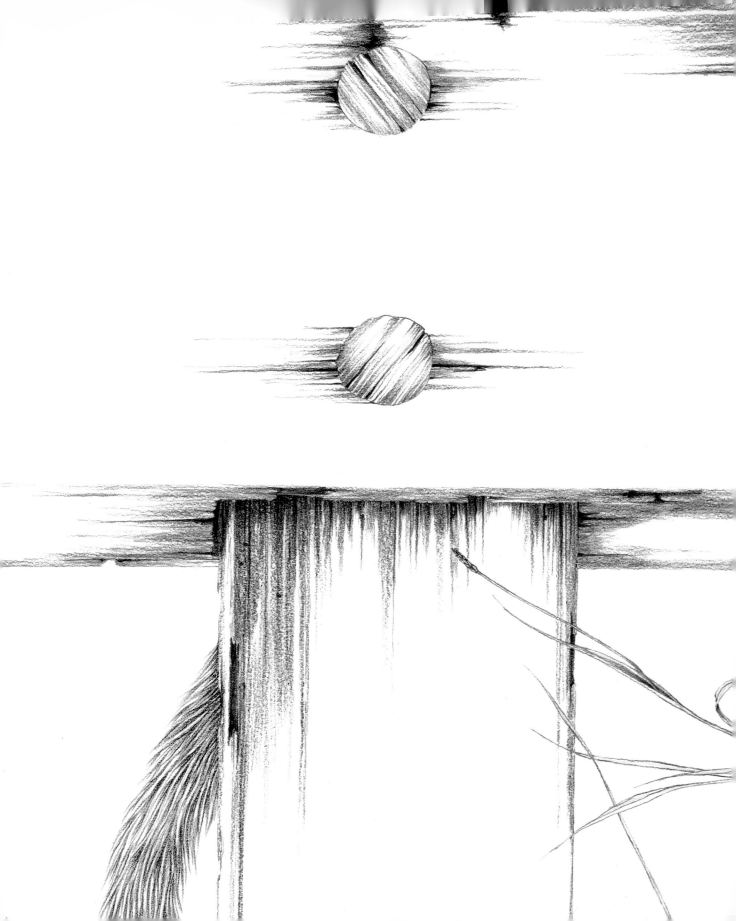

BLACKIE

Blackie was a wild, wild thing. When he came out of the marsh to prowl our land, a ghost was all we'd ever see. He moved to the barn from his old den tree when Winter made his whiskers twitch. Huge cat, wild cat—tame he could never be. He darted high in the loft...watching.

At lambing time two orphans struggled, ignored by ewes intent on their own new twins. I returned with a towel to dry them off and found Blackie there, draped over one and cleaning the other as though it was meant to be. For three days and nights he kept them warm but vanished when I brought them food. When the lambs gained strength, he returned to the loft till warmer days came, then returned to the marsh and his natural home.

I know where his den tree grows.

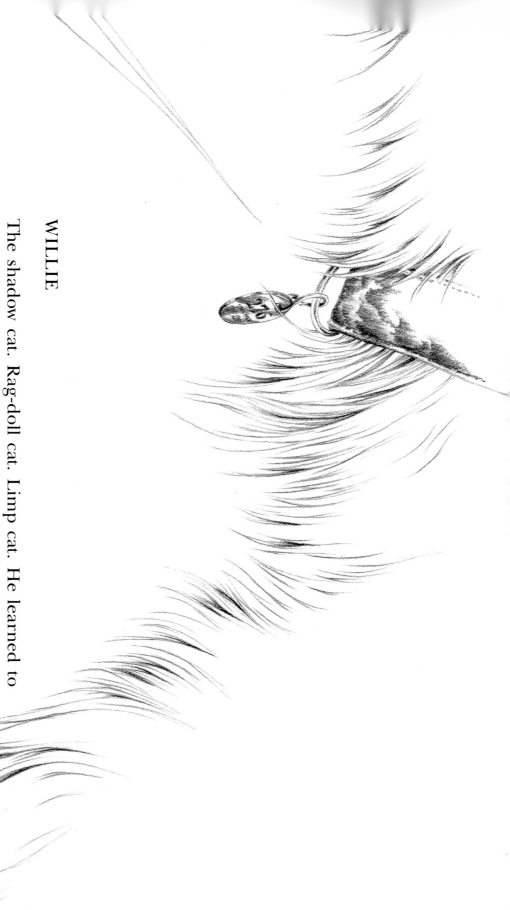

WILLIE

The shadow cat. Rag-doll cat. Limp cat. He learned to relax early in life when Dog cared for him, cleaned him, and called him "mine." Willie was carried on his various rounds by one hundred twenty pounds of tongue and teeth, with never a bruise to show. Shadows were his favorite toys, and a large one from a moving leaf replaced a bouncing ball...for Willie.

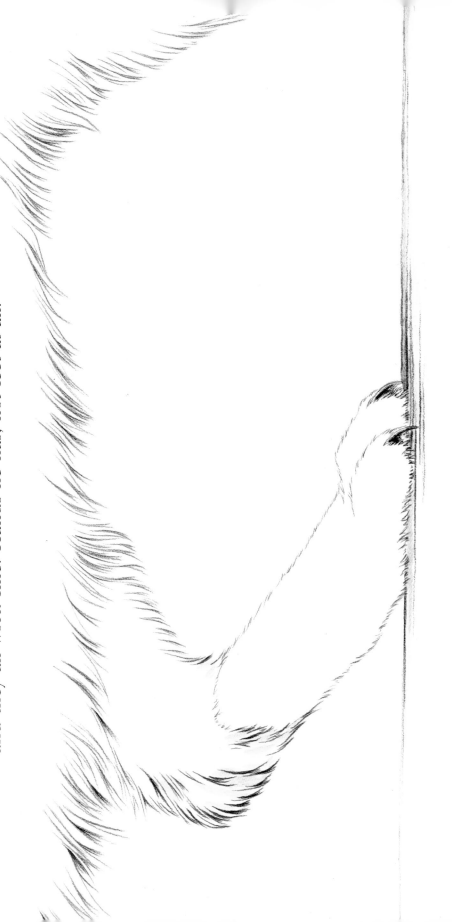

THUMBS

Thumbs walked up our lane one day with a mission in mind: to direct furry traffic on our farm. As soon as his first oversize foot stepped into our barn, he proceeded to do just that. None of our cats questions his word, for each front foot carries seven working toes, seven working claws, and they all work fine. Hands he has, not feet at all.

Thumbs came from Away, somewhere far, maybe Maryland or the great Northwest, for he purrs with an accent, I believe. He walks with us in the woods some days, and he answers back whenever we call.

"Thumbs?"

"*Rowrr!*"

"**Hey, Thumbs!**"

"*Rowrwrwr. Rowwrrrrrrr?*" And makes a question mark with his long, striped tail.

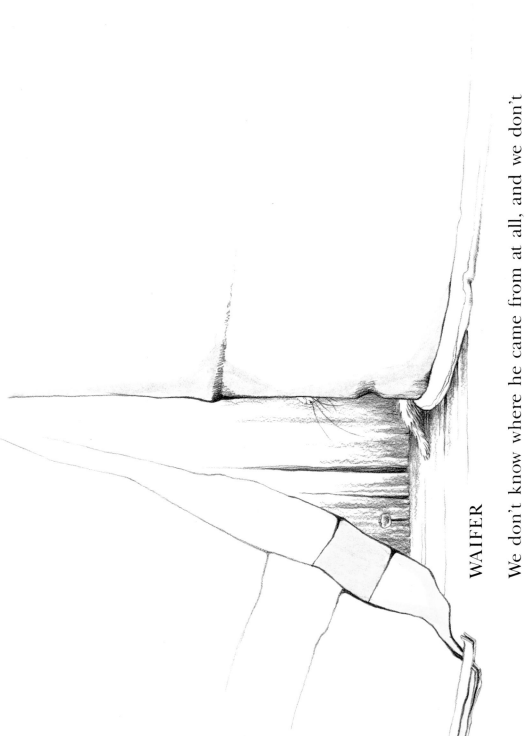

WAIFER

We don't know where he came from at all, and we don't know how he did. He showed up as a two-inch twitching tail peeking from behind a feed-room can. A waif from a far-off, unknown place. He came from Away…that mysterious place somewhere else, and stayed a long, long time.